Queen Elizabeth

A Biography of Queen Elizabeth

Table of Contents

Introduction

Thank you and congratulations for taking the time to pick up this book, documenting the fascinating life of Queen Elizabeth I.

This book aims to serve as a biography of the long-reigning Queen, covering topics such as how Queen Elizabeth came to be Queen in the first place, her political and religious views, and even discussing her much talked about romantic life.

Queen Elizabeth I made many changes to the United Kingdom during her reign. As you will learn in the following chapters, she was an incredibly forward thinking leader for her time, and her impact laid the foundations for life in the UK as we know it today.

Once again, thanks for choosing this book. I hope you find it to be both and enjoyable and informative read.

Chapter 1 – The Early Life of the Accidental Queen

From the moment she was born, Elizabeth's life was a troubled one.

Her father, Henry VIII, changed the course of England's history so that he could marry Anne Boleyn, hoping that this second marriage could produce a healthy and strong son, something he could not accomplish with Catherine of Aragon.

On September 7, 1533, Anne Boleyn gave birth to a princess named Elizabeth in Greenwich Palace. While Anne did eventually conceive a son, he was but a stillborn.

Henry VIII, by this point, began to grow weary of Anne and started to scheme her end. Historians agree that while his charges of Anne on adultery and incest were not true, it was all he needed to sign her warrant for execution.

Anne Boleyn was executed through beheading on May 19, 1536, at Tower Green, before Elizabeth was even three years old.

Following Anne's execution, Henry was married and was awaiting the son that Jane Seymour, his third wife, was carrying.

Jane Seymour, the Queen of England from 1536 to 1537, died shortly after the labor of her son Edward, who would become the future Edward VI.

Henry eventually married his sixth wife, Catherine Parr, who was Elizabeth's last stepmother. Catherine was to be the one who would restore Elizabeth and Mary, Elizabeth's stepsister, to Henry's court and into the line of succession. In 1547, when Henry VIII died, Catherine Parr married her final husband, Thomas Seymour.

Elizabeth and Queen Dowager Catherine had a good and close relationship but Elizabeth was sent away to live in Sir Anthony Denny's household in Cheshunt in May of 1548. Elizabeth was never to see her stepmother again.

The reasons as to why she was sent away were in part due to a possible scandal between Elizabeth and Thomas, Catherine Parr's then-husband. Apparently, Catherine found the two in an embrace. It has also been said that Elizabeth suffered emotional crisis due to Seymour's inappropriate sexual misconduct toward her. At this time, Catherine was also pregnant, which was a surprise. She gave birth to Mary, but died not too long afterward. She was buried in Sudeley Castle, making Thomas Seymour a suitable bachelor once more.

It is said that Catherine Parr's actions as regent, combined with her strength of character and noted dignity and religious convictions, were a significant influence on Lady Elizabeth, the future Queen of England.

Baptism & Education

Elizabeth was christened on September 10, 1533 by the Archbishop Thomas Cranmer. The Marques of Exeter, the Duchess of Norfolk, and the Dowager Marchioness of Dorset became her godparents.

Elizabeth was just about two years and eight months old when her mother, Anne Boleyn, was beheaded – only a mere four months after Catherine of Aragon's demise. The King's marriage to Anne was declared unacceptable and invalid through political machinations, and just like her sister Mary, Elizabeth too was pronounced illegitimate and dispossessed of her place in the lineup of succession.

Soon after Anne's execution, Henry married Jane Seymour, who would be only a stopgap before Elizabeth's four other step-mothers. Henry and Jane's son Edward was the undeniable heir apparent to the English crown.

Throughout her childhood and adulthood, Elizabeth was raised like any other child of royalty. She had several tutors and governesses. Among the first was Margaret Bryan who wrote about Elizabeth as a 'child of gentle conditions.' By 1537, Elizabeth was placed under the care of Blanche Herbert, Lady

Troy who was also the governess for half-sister Mary and half-brother Edward VI. Lady Troy remained Governess to Elizabeth I until her retirement in 1557, one-year shy of Elizabeth's accession to the throne.

Catherine Champernowne, better known as Kat Ashley, was then selected as the governess in 1537 and continued as Elizabeth's friend until Kat's death in 1565. Blanche Parry then became Chief Gentlewoman of the Privy Chambers. Through Parry, Elizabeth mastered four different languages, which were Italian, Spanish, Flemish and French.

Eventually, William Grindal became her tutor and by this time in 1544, Elizabeth could already speak Latin, Italian and English fluently. Grindal, however, was an experienced and talented teacher who further sharpened Elizabeth's knowledge in French and Greek.

In 1548, Grindal passed away, and Elizabeth continued her education with Roger Ascham, whose philosophy in learning was that it should be engaging. Elizabeth's formal education ended in 1550 and by this time, Elizabeth had risen to be one of the most intellectually powerful women of the period.

Elizabeth was also known to speak a little bit of Scottish, Irish, Cornish and even Welsh. In 1603, the Venetian Ambassador to England stated that Elizabeth "possessed languages so thoroughly that each appeared to be her native tongue."

<u>Succession to the Throne</u>

Elizabeth, being King Henry VIII's daughter, was undoubtedly next to the English throne, despite plenty of challenges to remove her from the succession. Henry VIII on the other hand had already included Elizabeth into his will as an heir.

Being in-line to the throne made Elizabeth a much-preferred bride. During King Edward VI's reign (he was crowned King at the age of nine), Thomas Seymour sought Elizabeth's hand in marriage, but she refused. Thomas Seymour was suspected of plotting against the King. Seymour, after a kidnapping attempt of the boy king, was arrested and eventually put to death on the Act of Attainder and was beheaded on 20 March 1549.

At the age of fifteen years old, Edward VI contracted what is now known as tuberculosis in February 1553. When it looked like the teenage King was doomed to die without an heir of his own, his and his Court drew up a succession to the Crown, in the hopes that the Crown would not pass down to his half-sister Mary, a professed Catholic.

Around that time, Guilford Dudley wedded Lady Jane Grey. Grey was a descendant of Mary, otherwise known as the sister of Henry VIII. This lineage also makes Lady Jane in line to the throne. When the boy-king Edward VI passed away, Jane was subsequently announced Queen, having been named the successor by Edward. Her father and father-in-law both would create massive militaries to support this.

Both Elizabeth and her half-sister were sidelined from the succession. Despite not being named in succession, many people supported the throne's rightful heir: Mary, the daughter from the union of Catherine of Aragon and King Henry VIII. Nine days after Lady Jane took up the throne of the Queen, the royal support that she had quickly fell away.

On the 3rd of August 1553, Elizabeth and Mary headed to London in triumph. Following the uprising, Jane and her husband were tucked away in the Tower of London as prisoners. Mary, now the Queen of England, was determined to squash out any Protestant influence and even made her sister Elizabeth profess outwardly. There was plenty of Protestant persecution going on during this time.

However, in 1554, Queen Mary's popularity began to wane especially when she announced her marriage to the Prince of Spain, Phillip. Unrest and discord were spreading throughout England because of Prince Philip's staunch Catholicism, and everyone looked towards Elizabeth as their savior.

There were a massive number of rebellions conducted in the name of Queen Elizabeth such as the Wyatt Rebellion. Having no hand in this whatsoever, Mary sensed the danger at hand and subsequently imprisoned Elizabeth in the Tower on 18 March, making Elizabeth yet another famous prisoner of the Tower.

Elizabeth was sent to Woodstock after a few months in the Tower. Here she stayed for a year. During this time, Mary was apparently pregnant, and Elizabeth was seen as no significant threat should Mary conceive a child. Elizabeth was sent to return to her court so that she could be there for Mary during the final stages of her pregnancy. However, after significant delay and many months, it seemed that Mary had a false pregnancy, despite a protruding belly, probably due to her intense desire to have a child.

However, modern medicine states that it could be that Mary had an enormous, untreated ovarian cyst, which could have been the reason for her failing health and ultimate death.

At this point, Elizabeth's succession seemed apparent. Prince Phillip, on the other hand, became the latest political reality and the increasing popularity of Elizabeth concluded that Elizabeth was a far better political partner to have than Mary, Queen of Scots.

On 6 November 1556, Mary named Elizabeth as heir to the throne, and by November 15, 1558, Mary had succumbed to death, leaving Elizabeth to ascend to the throne.

What this meant was that Elizabeth had survived her rough road to the throne and was finally made Queen of England. Queen Elizabeth made her procession to Westminster on the 14th of January and ended up staying overnight in the Palace of Westminster. The very next day, Elizabeth walked to the Abbey for her royal coronation greeted with much oration and celebration, alongside the deafening noise of trumpets, bells, and drums.

The coronation of Queen Elizabeth I took place, only two months after Mary died, on January 15, 1559 by Owen Oglethorpe, the bishop of Carlisle at Westminster Abbey. The coronation mass included readings of both Latin and English, and after the coronation, Queen Elizabeth walked elated and victorious to the Westminster Hall for her coronary banquet.

She was made Queen of England at age 25. In her coronation speech, Elizabeth made it clear that she would rule with 'two bodies,' one of the body natural and the other of the body politic.

Marriage Proposals

Elizabeth again became an eligible bachelorette, and following her coronation and ascension to the throne, plenty of suitors were vying for her hand.

It could be said that the reason Elizabeth never married was that the experiences with Thomas Seymour put her off any sexual relationship. Queen Elizabeth continued to entertain suitors till she was 50, but as we know it, she remained unmarried and childless.

Some theories revolve around how King George VIII, the father of Elizabeth, treated his wives, which caused Elizabeth to be absolutely disillusioned with marriage entirely. Other theories were related to her love towards her childhood friend, Lord Robert Dudley whom she could not marry.

Robert Dudley

Robert Dudley, at the time, was already a married man. When it started to become clear that Elizabeth had fallen for Dudley, the agreement was struck that she would marry him should his wife, Amy die. At this point, Amy was suffering from something which in all likelihood could have been breast cancer.

Amy died of a 'misfortunate accident' which then created a massive scandal suggesting that Robert Dudley instigated the killing of his wife, although there was absolutely no hard evidence. The scandal suggested that Robert arranged for the death of his wife so he could marry the Queen.

Because of this, Elizabeth was warned by her court which included William Cecil, Nicholas Throckmorton, and other conservative peers against the marriage. There was even a rumor that suggested the gentry of England would rise if the wedding happened.

Due to this standing, Elizabeth did not continue with the idea of marrying Dudley. Despite this, going on for more than the next ten years, Dudley was still considered to be a possible suitor. In 1564, the Queen raised Dudley's peerage to become Earl of Leicester.

In 1578, Dudley remarried, and the Queen crystallized a lifelong hatred towards Lettice Knollys, his wife.

Robert Dudley however, remained Queen Elizabeth's favorite and continued to be the center of her emotional life. He died of malaria on 4 September 1588, with his wife Lettice by his side. According to historian Susan Doran, upon Elizabeth's death, a note penned by Dudley had been found amongst her things. This note was marked 'his last letter' in her handwriting.

Regardless of what reason Elizabeth did not marry, she successfully played off her suitors for the next 25 years, at the same time gaining their alliances and receiving expensive gifts.

Francis, Duke of Alencon

Another serious contender for Elizabeth's hand in marriage was the Duke of Alencon of France. The Duke was the youngest son of Henry II of France and Catherine de' Medici. The Duke is the only person among all of Elizabeth's suitors to court her in person. At this time, Elizabeth was 46 years old and the Duke only 24. It is unclear whether Elizabeth truly planned on marrying the Duke, but it was very obvious that she was very fond of him, often referring to him as her 'frog.' She probably played out the engagement knowing that the Duke of Anjou was probably the last of her suitors. Elizabeth eventually did not see the union as wise, despite her Privy Court which encouraged it.

A poem she penned after his departure in 1581 entitled 'On Monsieur's Departure' has given many historians and Elizabethan enthusiasts the idea that she might have been willing to marry him after all.

The Golden Age

The final years of Elizabeth's sovereignty would become to be known as the Golden Age. At this point in time, Elizabeth and England faced many trials. Firstly, Elizabeth dealt with the imminent threat of Mary, Queen of Scots who, in the eyes of the Catholics was the legitimate and rightful heir to the English Throne. When Mary made her escape in 1560, she was placed under house arrest in England. While in England, she thought she would have total security from Elizabeth, being that Elizabeth was her cousin. Elizabeth, however, knew that Mary was a major threat to her and signed her death warrant. Mary was executed on 8 February 1587.

Apart from this, Elizabeth also faced many military threats, especially from the Spanish Armada. During this war, England would end up winning. As a result, it paved its own path to being one of the most dominant naval powers in the world during the 1600s and 1700s when colonization under the crown began to materialize.

During the last period of her sovereignty, Elizabeth was trying to navigate an increasing number of obstacles, largely in the form of the Puritan pressure and the revolt from the Earl of Essex, Robert Devereux.

Death and Succession of the Throne

Queen Elizabeth I passed away on 24 March 1603 at Richmond Palace at the age of 69. She was succeeded by James I, who was also at the time known as James VI of Scotland.

James I is the son of Mary, Queen of Scots. The death of Elizabeth I and the succession by James I marked the end of the Tudor monarchy and the beginning of the Stuart Dynasty. According to the will left behind by Henry VIII, the next heir to the throne after Henry's children are the remaining daughters of Frances Brandon, daughter of Henry VIII's sister, Mary Tudor.

As we know, Lady Jane Grey, the first daughter of Frances, was executed during Mary's reign after being on the throne for only nine days after Edward VI's death. Jane also had two other sisters by the names of Catherine and Mary Grey. After Elizabeth had taken the throne, it appeared that Catherine was the legal successor to the throne of England.

However, since Catherine Grey wedded Edward Seymour (son of the Lord Protector) without the consent of Elizabeth, her marriage to Seymour was declared unacceptable, thus meaning that neither Catherine nor her children could succeed Elizabeth.

Catherine would end up dying in 1568, and so she posed no threat to Elizabeth's succession in 1603. The fact that the last two remaining children of France's died, the line of succession fell to her two sons - Edward and Thomas.

The line of succession after Edward and Thomas would be Mary Grey's children but despite being married, Mary Grey would never have any children and would actually die many years before Elizabeth would.

The brood of Margaret Tudor, married to James IV of Scotland, was not declared as part of the line of succession since they were both born overseas. Although, they were successors of the eldest daughter of Henry VII which, according to succession rules, means that they technically had a stronger vie for the crown than any of Mary's descendants.

During the final days of Elizabeth's life, it seems that the most valid conclusion for succession would be James VI of Scotland. Elizabeth, before her death had secret dealings with her government to determine the next in line for the crown, which paved the way for James I succession.

In modern historical developments, nobody still really knows if Elizabeth named James to be her successor or not. However, it could be possible that Elizabeth never officially specified James as the rightful heir in black and white because of the state of affairs of her sister's demise and the fact that the people had forsaken Mary for her.

Regardless of whether she indicated James as her heir, it was eventually the King of Scotland that succeeded the throne peacefully, despite other claims to the throne.

While plenty lamented her death, some of her countrymen and subjects were relieved by it. Elizabeth was seen as the ruler of the Golden Age and a heroine among the Protestants. Her reign was instrumental in the raising of England's status globally and thus gained a new confidence to the people and a sense of sovereignty.

Elizabeth's long reign as queen saw a strong and unified England. Her death signified the unification of England and Scotland under one crown.

To Sum It Up

Marriage and death played a huge part in determining the next in line, and more often than not, wars were fought, and marriages were made to seal a binding contract and secure the line to the throne.

In the following chapters, we will discuss more on other aspects of Elizabeth's life such as her political views, assassination attempts towards her life, her impact, as well as her legacy.

Chapter 2- Assassination Attempts towards the Queen

Queen Elizabeth I was no doubt a woman who had many lucky breaks.

As with many important figures and heads of a country, assassination attempts were nothing new for Kings and Queens. Nobody is every satisfied with a ruling monarch at any given time.

This was especially true for Elizabeth I since not everyone agreed that she was the legitimate heir, let alone a legitimate child to Henry VIII.

Not only that, some quarters wanted Mary, Queen of Scots to ascend the throne and restore Catholicism.

Even back then, religion was always a major dividing force among people.

Among the achievements of Elizabeth I is how she got to be Queen and by doing so, managed to not only make it past her illegitimacy but also managed to live long enough in order to actually take up the throne from Mary I.

Elizabeth herself probably did not keep any kind of desires to take the throne, especially since she had two older siblings ahead of her and in line to the throne. But as history would have its way, Elizabeth was destined to be Queen, whether accidental or not.

A country divided was unified under Elizabeth but unfortunately, greed always gets the better of men hence the numerous assassination attempts on her.

During Mary I's reign, Elizabeth's life was often dangerous. At this time, Elizabeth was linked with the Wyatt Rebellion, an uprising with the objective of overthrowing Mary I and replacing her with Elizabeth. Despite becoming Queen, Elizabeth's life was still under threat. There were plenty of other assassination attempts against the Queen, and Elizabeth surviving it and above all, having a long and successful reign (without a King on top of that) is an achievement on its own.

There was also constant danger from Pope Pius V against Elizabeth, especially in the form of the Bull Regnans in Excelsis of Excommunications and Deposition against Elizabeth in 1570. This Papal Bull gave explicit permission to Catholics to revolt against Elizabeth and even attempt to kill her. This led to the implementation of incredibly anti-Catholic laws by Elizabeth, her court, and the English government.

Here are some of the known and infamous assassination attempts:

1) The Somerville Assassination Attempt

Back in 1583 in December, Elizabeth I penned a letter to the French Ambassador. Her words were "There are more than two hundred men of all ages who, at the instigation of the Jesuits, conspire to kill me." Her words echoed her fear when in October 1583, Elizabeth's life was yet again threatened by John Somerville from Warwickshire. Being a Catholic, John had been stirring up anti-Elizabeth propaganda which began first with the Jesuit priests.

Somerville set out to assassinate Queen Elizabeth with a pistol, with the objective of seeing "her head on a pole, for she was a serpent and a viper". This assassination stab failed however as he was detained and then condemned to execution a little before he was able to slay the Queen. Somerville, however, would kill himself in his prison cell before his execution could be carried out.

2) The William Parry Assassination Attempt

A year after the Somerville incident, Elizabeth I had another threat in the form of would-be assassin William Parry. Parry was a Welsh MP who hid in the Queen's garden and was planning to assassinate her but lost his courage when he saw her, stating he was "so daunted with the majesty of her presence in which he saw the image of her father, King Henry VIII".

It remains unclear if Parry actually intended to kill the Queen or was doing it to gain fame. William Cecil and Lord Burleigh knew Parry and knew that he did work as a spy. However, Parry was known to boast that if he had the chance, he would assassinate Elizabeth. Parry was sentenced to death at the gallows.

3) The Barge Incident

Among the famous attempts of the Elizabethan assassination was while Elizabeth was traveling by the barge at River Thames. While walking, a gunshot broke the air, and one of the crewmen on the barge was struck by it, causing him to bleed to death. Elizabeth gave him her hankie to place on his injury, stating "Be of good cheer, for you will never want. For the bullet was meant for me."

4) The Ridolfi Plot

This plot happened in 1571 with the objective of assassinating Elizabeth so that Mary, Queen of Scots could replace her. Mary at that time was to be married to the fourth Duke of Norfolk, Thomas Howard. The name of the plot comes from Roberto Ridolfi, a papal agent from Florence who would fund a Northern Catholic resistance within England, and an attack from Philip of Spain. Thankfully due to Sir Francis Walsingham's undercover spy network, this plot was uncovered and collapsed. Thomas Howard was immediately executed in 1572 and after the event, Elizabeth would nevermore trust Mary, the Queen of Scots.

5) The Throgmorton Plot

Another attempt on Elizabeth I's life was in 1583, again with the intention of replacing her with Mary, Queen of Scots. Named after Francis Throgmorton, this attempt involved Throgmorton serving as an intermediate between Queen Mary and her agent Thomas Morning, as well as Don Bernardino de Mendoza, the Spanish Ambassador. The spy network of Sir Francis Walsingham heard about the plot and immediately put Throgmorton under arrest. During his trial and "investigation", he would let loose the information that the Duke of Guise intended to hold an invasion of the Netherlands. Throgmorton was subsequently executed, and Mendoza thrown out of England.

6) The Babington Plot

In 1586, the final major attempt against Elizabeth's life was had, also centering around Mary, Queen of Scots. It was named after Anthony Babington who was under the Queen of Scot's employ. He established a secret society which would serve to assist the Jesuits who were entering England. The plot had the Pope's blessing. Again, Walsingham proved to be an invaluable asset to Elizabeth I and uncovered the plot, in the process saving Elizabeth's life once more. John Ballard, the Jesuit priest who cooked up the scheme, was arrested, tortured, and then executed. Babington was also executed as a traitor in September 1586.

By the time the Babington assassination attempt took place, Queen Elizabeth's patience had waned on Roman Catholics and with Mary, Queen of Scots. Mary was then executed in 1587, after nearly a 20-year house arrest in England.

Part of the success of curtailing any assassination attempts to the Queen was due to the expert underground spy network created by Sir Francis Walsingham. You can even say that it was a little bit of luck and fate that things worked in favor of the queen.

Whatever the reason, Elizabeth survived it all and lived to rule England and bring it to prosperity, peace, and stability, and for it to become one of the greatest countries in medieval times.

Chapter 3 – Queen Elizabeth's Beliefs and Politics

When Elizabeth's reign began in 1558, it was understood that one of her first's roles as Queen would be to restore Protestantism throughout England. At the very early stages of her reign, it was becoming very evident that Elizabeth faced a huge challenge brought on by two contrasting fronts. The first came from the hardcore Catholics who willed to carry on the work of her sister, Mary I. The second front came in the form of Protestants who wanted a more radical approach to the Church of England.

Catholics during this time worked in a more secretive way to avoid persecution, whereas the Protestants headed towards more radicalized approaches. Most Protestants returned to England after Mary's death and expected a change of progress from Elizabeth.

The persecution of Protestants during Mary's reign yielded damage to the Catholic community in England because the number of Protestants, despite the persecution, continue to rise steadily. Elizabeth has been raised a Protestant, despite deeming herself a Catholic while Mary I reigned.

She held a strong conviction to Christianity, and her religious views were astonishingly tolerant and forward for the generation that she ruled and lived in. Elizabeth believed and was steadfast in her faith but at the same time believed in religious tolerance, stating that both Protestants and Catholics are people who share the same essential belief in Christ.

She proclaimed that "There is only one Christ, Jesus, one faith - all else is a dispute over trifles."

All throughout her reign in England, her primary concern was the stability of her kingdom and the peace of her people. Many others alive at the time, however, did not have the same set of forward-thinking views, and by circumstance, she had no choice other than to take up harsher rules on Catholics – more than she had ever desired. Elizabeth restored Protestantism as the official religion in England but also believed that people should have the freedom to practice the Catholic religion without fearing recrimination. This is allowed as long as there was no threat to the peace of her people and her reign over England.

Despite this forward tolerance, there were still plenty of plots to overthrow or assassinate the Queen. Many Catholics still focused on getting Mary, Queen of Scots to the throne, which eventually led to the execution of Mary.

1559 Religious Settlement

This settlement that was drawn up under Elizabeth's ruling was known as the Elizabethan Settlement. It was developed in the 'via media' way which means a middle way to outline and define the Church of England. Under this settlement, the Church of England is moderately Reformed in doctrine, as mentioned in the Thirty-Nine Articles and it also emphasized the continuation of the Apostolic and Catholic traditions according to the Church Fathers.

The Settlement also states that the Church of England is an established church - one that has been established constitutionally by the state, and the head of state is the supreme governor. This settlement and its defined nature of the connection between Church and Crown would be a continued source of friction for the next oncoming century.

The Church and Protestantism under Elizabeth I

Several changes took place in England during Elizabeth's reign. Some of these were connected to the way people prayed, preached, and attended service. When Queen Elizabeth began her reign, she inherited a nation that was suffering from religious flux. However, at the end of her reign, England stood more proud, and it paved the way to a stronger, stable nation.

The Reformation of Henry VIII, her father, made the monarchy the spiritual and secular head of the kingdom, was continued by Henry's son and Elizabeth's half-brother, Edward VI. When Queen Mary I took over, this was reversed, and England in 1553 became Roman Catholic, and the Pope became the head of church once again.

It was common at that time for any kingdom or state to follow the religion of the ruler at the time.

Once Queen Elizabeth I took her reign, she paved the way for a reasonable religious settlement that was an extension of her father's break from Rome. Elizabeth I then established the Church of England in 1559.

- **Church Services and the Bible**

  - During Elizabeth's reign, Catholics at that time firmly believed that services or mass, as well as the Bible, must be in Latin, as it had been for the past 1000 years.

  - However, the Protestants held the belief that both Church services and the Bible itself should be in the vernacular of the people, so that people from any education background, whether literate or illiterate could understand what was being preached to them.

- **The Priests**

  - During her reign, Elizabethan Catholics held the belief that Priests were the ultimate link between the people and God, and also that the Pope was a chosen person by God.

  - Catholic priests were seen as people that devoted their whole lives to God, thus making them special vessels of Christ. Priests under the Catholic faith remained unmarried and celibate, and they wore elaborate vestments.

- The Protestants view was that people could find God without going through the Pope or a priest.

- Ministers or Pastors were ordinary folks that, in their eyes, should have led ordinary lives, wearing common clothing.

- **Sins**

    - The Catholics believe that the priests and pope, being the intermediary between God and his people, could seek forgiveness for sins. This practice eventually came at a price due to priests abusing this right and asking for indulgences, which were essentially tithes made to the Church in order to absolve somebody of their sins.

    - Protestants believed that God and God alone could actually absolve somebody of their sins.

- **Churches**

    - The Catholics believed that human capacity for beauty was a gift from God itself, and so the churches were very ornate.

    - Protestants, on the other hand, believed that Churches should be plain and simple, to allow its people to concentrate on the sermons.

The above are the major differences between the Elizabethan Catholics and the Elizabethan Protestants doctrine, prayer style, and beliefs.

Elizabeth's policies and role in defining the Church of England could be identified in the following ways:

A) Building a peaceful and stable nation

Elizabeth had always wanted to see England become a peaceful nation - one with a strong government and free from foreign influence, especially where the state and the church are concerned. To realize this vision, it was imperative to enable a new religious settlement that made religious inclusion as best as could be.

Elizabeth knew that changes were required, but these changes needed minimum confrontation on both ends of the faith spectrum in England so that there would be no fear of England's people and less suspicion from powers abroad. England needed an official religion and choosing one would have political consequences, no matter which side she chose.

If Elizabeth chose to remain Catholicism as the state religion, then that would mean surrendering its faith power to Rome, making England an ally with other powerful Catholic majority countries such as France and Spain.

However, remaining to Protestantism would make England an ally with the Dutch, who at that time were her most important trading partner. This would also mean pricking Spain, which was the world's most powerful nation with a strong armada at that point.

Declaring Protestantism as the official religion might also strike the fear of persecution into the Catholics, which may lead to riots or uprising.

B) Building a prosperous and united country

The first Parliament sitting under Elizabeth's reign was on 25 January 1559. The opening speech was given by Nicholas Bacon, the Lord Keeper of the Privy Seal. Bacon, as a spokesperson for the Elizabethan government, delivered the mission statement, reinforcing their aim 'to unite the people of this realm into a uniform order of religion.'

To reach this ultimate goal, Bacon outlined to Parliament that members will not participate in insulting each other using terms such as 'heretic' 'Papist' and even 'schismatic.' Parliament was also not going to waste time in theological debates but rather focus its attention on finding strong solutions to the country's present problems.

Issues also had to be debated in an orderly and respectful fashion and under no circumstances would extremism be tolerated. This also included no mud-slinging and name calling. Elizabeth, in this address delivered by Bacon, sought to disassociate herself from the very unpopular regime of Queen Mary I, thus giving out a strong signal that things moving forward, would be different under her rule.

C) Constructing a new religious settlement

In February 1559, the House of Commons passed the first act together with the bill of supremacy, which established Queen Elizabeth I as the head of the church. This proposed settlement was rejected and subsequently adulterated by the Catholic-majority House of Lords.

Another strategy was needed, so Elizabeth and her pro-reform ministers had to plan again. During the Easter recess, a debate was scheduled between the Catholic team and the Protestant team. The judge of this debate was the Privy Council, and the Chairperson was Mr. Nicholas Bacon himself. This debate, although starting off with all good intentions, quickly turned into a name-calling drama and two Catholics were sent to the Tower for contempt.

D) The Act of Supremacy

This debate, however, became a sort of enlightenment for Elizabeth and her counselors as they learned not to misjudge the opposition. Come April, Parliament convened again, and issues were presented to members separately, and substantial concessions were undertaken.

The Act of Supremacy was revised, and it maintained the abolishing of Papal supremacy, but defined the Queen as the Supreme Governor of the Church.

The change of title from Supreme Head to Supreme Governor was received well by those who thought that a woman could not hold a position as the head of the church. Thus, the act was passed considerably easily in Parliament.

E) The Act of Uniformity

This Act provided the foundation for the Elizabethan church. Not only did it enable the restoration of the 1552 version of the English Prayer Book but it also retained many of the old and familiar practices that allowed for two communion rites interpretation which were the Catholic version and the Protestant version.
Although the Act was hotly debated at first, it was eventually passed in Parliament in 1559 by an extra three votes.

Government and Politics

The Elizabethan England materialized into an incredibly structured society, but with a slightly complicated system of government. The Government of England had two national bodies, which were the Privy Council and the Parliament. After this came the regional bodies, which were the Council of the Marches and the North. This was followed by local counties and community institutions.

The central government consisted of:
- The Monarchy
- The Privy Council
- The Parliament

These three bodies worked effectively together like well-oiled cogs to reign, to create legislature, to raise funds for the government affairs, and to decide on matters of national defense and religion. The Privy Council was essentially an administrative branch that only oversaw the administrative duties and government issues for all of then-Britain.

Local Government

In Tudor England, local government was critical, hence the Council of the North, and the Council of the Marches worked with a more localized approach in government affairs. To make certain that all of the Queen's statutes and the English law itself were adhered to, the Queen's court had royal representatives in nearly every single county.

The most critical of royal representatives were the Justices of Peace, the Sheriffs, and also the Lord Lieutenants. In each city and town, they had their own hierarchical system, and there were also other officials whose jobs were to keep an eye on certain matters. The mayor was the principal officer.

The Nobility and Gentry

The nobility and the gentry had a significant influence in Tudor and Elizabethan times. The ones who possessed great power and influence also had great wealth. They were masters of their tenants and the owners of the land and all who worked it.

The nobility and gentry crowd were looked upon as being very important figures. Additionally, they were supposed to help the monarch regnant with managing and governing the land that they presided over. The lords of the land are where the local folk took their grievances to. Some of the gentry and noble folk took this job seriously and went to the extent of establishing institutions of education and religion.

The vassals, as part of the tenancy contract, were to have absolute loyalty for their lords, and if the lords wanted war, the vassals had to go fight. The nobility could command the loyalty of a significant population of their land or county, which is why the Tudor monarchy was afraid of too. Politics and religion were deeply critical and required the influence of the noble and gentry.

Courts of the Land

Another aspect of England's governmental system was the system of English courts. The most critical courts were the Great Session, held twice a year in every county, and the Quarter Sessions Court, held four times a year. These two courts would be the ones to handle various crimes from theft to murder, assault, and witchcraft.

The crime of High Treason, however, was commonly handled at the hands of the royal court - the Queen and her Council - and it usually ended with a death sentence. Crimes which were less egregious were normally resultant in a punishment of either imprisonment or a certain amount of time in the stocks. Sometimes, a person would get both.

Monarch

Elizabethan England was so much more different back then compared to now. Queen Elizabeth had her ball in every single court of the English territory, which is drastically different from the roles played by today's monarch regnants, who are more of icons and symbols than decision-makers in politics and the government. Despite being a ruler, the Queen or King even back then was not above the law. In fact, they had to act in agreement with the law, which made governing a country justly and wisely much more transparent.

Elizabeth, as Queen, could have a say in:

- The official religion of England
- When parliament should go into session and what could be discussed
- When the country can go to war
- Matters related to education
- The welfare of the people
- Choosing her councilors and advisors who would help her to run England
- Sending men and women to prison and ordering executions

Not obeying the Queen meant that a person was going against the law which counted as treason and, well, the penalty was death. Some men and women became powerful and influential just by being associated or in a close acquaintanceship or connection with Queen Elizabeth.

Privy Council

The Queen, for the most part, would avoid much of the day-to-day dirty work, which would rather fall into the hands of this council. Who sat on this Council, though, was entirely in the hands of Queen Elizabeth I. However, Elizabeth also made her choice taking into consideration the influence and money that the lords had in their counties, or risk rebellion against her.

Elizabeth reduced her council from fifty members to nineteen members because she felt too many people brought too many different ideas and made things hard to deal with. The council could issue proclamations under the Queen's name and also supervised statutes enforcement. The council was also responsible for advising Elizabeth whenever she needed, and while they did not always agree, she would always give fair credence to all particular points of view before finally coming to a conclusion herself.

William Cecil

The council traditionally would only meet thrice per week, but by the time that Elizabeth's time on the throne was drawing to an end, the council was meeting almost every day. The council delegated their work to secretaries and among the most famous was William Cecil, the Secretary of State who would also serve as the leader of the council. The Secretary of State was also Queen Elizabeth's personal secretary. William Cecil was an influential man with administrative abilities that were so great it earned him the reputation of one of England's greatest political leaders.

William Cecil was chief advisor to Elizabeth till his death in 1598. Elizabeth and William had an excellent working relationship, and she trusted him above all her councilors and advisors. Some historians attribute Elizabeth's successful regime to the wisdom and acumen that resulted from the working relationship of Elizabeth and William.

Parliament

The Tudor Parliament was built up of two different houses: The House of Lords, and the House of Commons. In this way, it's very much like today's parliament. Elections were conducted for the House of Commons, and it was only men who could vote. Parliament's main function was to verify legislation and to give the Queen funding whenever she found herself in need of it. Back then, the Queen could create and verify legislation even without the agreeing of the standing Parliament. This was called Royal Proclamations, and the Queen only resorted to such proclamations if she and the Privy Council were unable to convince Parliament to pass an issue.

The Parliament back then did not have much power back in the Tudor Monarchy compared to the power it has now. The Queen was the one who summoned the Parliament to a sitting, and it was usually for major governmental reforms or most often than not, for money. There was also no Prime Minister or political parties present at this time.

Chapter 4- Queen Elizabeth I's Impact as Queen

Queen Elizabeth's accomplishments and achievements astounded many, especially since she was never seen as a likely heir to the throne. Because of her accomplishments and successful reign, she earned the esteem of many as the best monarch England has ever had.

The Elizabethan Era is also referred to as the Golden Age, for many reasons. How did one Queen, an unlikely successor to the throne, bring about such a monumental change in England?

Major Accomplishments

- **Survival**

As described in previous chapters, her survival to become Queen, let alone the longest reigning one at that time, was a major accomplishment in itself. From her mother being executed only when she was two years old, to being branded illegitimate, losing her place in court and her title Princess Elizabeth, surviving incest and possible adultery and surviving plenty of assassination attempts - Queen Elizabeth has been there, done that.

- **Education, Literature, and Arts**

Elizabeth received a level of education that most women her age and status would have received. However, Elizabeth was far more gifted as a scholar, and she was also an accomplished linguist, having been able to speak in a huge number of different tongues fluently, such as Greek, French, Spanish, Latin, and Welsh.

Because of this, Elizabeth sought to pave the way to ensure that her people had access to education. During her reign, there was a massive upturn in the English literacy rate, and the advancement of the arts grew as well at this point. Many literature greats, poets, and artists emerged during the Golden

Era, including the ever famous figures William Shakespeare and Sir Walter Raleigh. Writers and artists paid tribute to her in many ways.

- **Science**

During Elizabeth's reign, the new scientific thinking flourished together with the Renaissance movement. This new age thinking brought forward men such as Sir Francis Bacon, who would develop very sophisticated philosophical ideas, and Dr. John Dee, a skillful mathematician, astronomer, and advisor to the Queen. It also encouraged a more sophisticated spying network, in particular through the likes of Sir Francis Walsingham.

- **Government Relations**

Elizabeth developed an acute sense of public relations through the many suitors that desired to marry her in order to become King. Elizabeth used these connections to forge stronger ties with her foreign counterparts, bring in wealth, and above all to create a stable country.

- **Military Strength**

During Elizabeth's reign, England saw its major military accomplishment in defeating the Spanish Armada of 132 with only 34 English naval ships and 163 armed merchant vessels, led by Lord Howard of Effingham, Sir John Hawkins, and Sir Francis Drake. The English Navy also stamped out future invasion attempts.

- **Trade & Voyages**

Queen Elizabeth granted or gave permission to many trade ships to travel out beyond the European realm in search for trading routes and spices.

Elizabeth's reign witnessed a steady rise in English exploration, which brought about the expansion of English influence, subsequently leading to the formation of the British Empire.

In 1600, the British East India Company was founded, and on 31 December that same year, Queen Elizabeth gave the Royal Charter to continue expansion and discovery and control of the spice trade. Francis Drake would end up becoming the first Englishman to sail around the entire world.

The trades and voyages made England a powerhouse in Europe.

• Religious Tolerance and Welfare

Elizabeth was a woman way ahead of her time. Even back in her reign, Elizabeth knew the importance of religious tolerance. Her moderate religious policy gave way to the Acts of Supremacy and Uniformity (1559) as well as the reinstating of the 1559 Prayer Book and the Thirty-Nine Articles in 1563. While they were all Protestant in doctrine, they were still a preservation of traditional Catholic ceremonies.

She did not persecute Catholics the way her half-sister Mary I did. She, being a Protestant, established Protestantism as the official English religion in her reign and further enabled the increase of Anglicans.

Queen Elizabeth also developed the Poor Laws, which created a much-needed system that allowed the support and funding for the needy.

• A Woman in a Man's World

Queen Elizabeth I, as a young lady led England in many ways breaking the glass ceiling. While everyone expected her to marry and marry soon, in the hopes of continuing her bloodline and producing an heir, preferably male, Elizabeth instead little by little broke boundaries as each year kept passing by. She broke barriers with courage, resilience, intelligence, and loyalty.

She chose a different path - to become Queen in her own right, to exercise her power, and establish herself as a unique power at that. During a time when it was thought that women were weak and unsuited to rule, there she was, standing out different, and became an icon for it.

Queen Elizabeth showed symbolic power and intelligence, charisma and precision - this became the foundation of her endurance through her 44 years of reign.

Elizabeth may have been an accidental Queen. She may not have been a ruler that England desired or wanted, but she definitely became a Queen that England needed.

Chapter 5- Pivotal Moments in Queen Elizabeth I's Reign

Throughout Elizabeth's reign, England became a force to be reckoned with. There were many pivotal moments during her reign, most of them signaling a change of direction, creating a new beginning and overall defining a new wave in terms of how the English led their lives.

Here is a timeline of the many different pivotal moments during her 44 years of reign:

1558	- On November 17, Queen Elizabeth ascends the throne - Becomes successor to Mary I - Replaced the Catholic Church with the Anglican Church, undoing Catholic laws along the way.
1559	- Elizabeth is made Queen of England
1560	- English troops lay siege to the French at Leith - July 6, the Treaty of Edinburgh among England, Scotland and France is signed
1560	- September 8- Robert Dudley's partner found suspiciously deceased
1561	- August 19- Mary, Queen of Scots, returns to Scotland after the demise of her husband, King Francis II - September 20- Elizabeth pledges support for the French Huguenots through a treaty signed at Hampton Court
1562	- July 15- Elizabeth refuses to meet Mary, Queen of Scots, due to Mary's constant attacks against the French Protestants. - Elizabeth contracts smallpox, nearly dies
1565	- Mary, Queen of Scots, marries The Lord Darnley
1566	- March 9 - David Rizzio, private secretary to

	Mary, Queen of Scots, murdered by Mary's husband Lord Darnley. - Jun 19 – Mary has her sole child, James
1567	- Feb. 10 – Lord Darnley is murdered - Months later, Mary would proceed to marry James Hepburn, causing disapproval and rebellion - May 15, Mary is imprisoned in Loch Leven Castle - Jul. 24, 1567 - Mary is forced to abdicate the Scottish throne and her one year old son, James, becomes King James VI of Scotland
1568	- May 2 - Mary escaped from Loch Leven - May 16 - Leaves Scotland by fishing boat, enters England - The Catholic Mary, Queen of Scots, kept under house arrest at Fotheringay Castle
1569	- Elizabeth vindicates Mary, Queen of Scots, from assassination charges made toward her - Oct 1, - Thomas Howard, Duke of Norfolk is ordered to be retained for a secret plot to wed Mary, Queen of Scots
1570	- Elizabeth I is excommunicated by the Catholic Church
1571	- Jan 2 – Elizabeth and Henry, Duke of Anjou start preparing plans and conditions in order to marry - Feb 25, 1571 - Sir William Cecil is elevated to Baron and became Lord Burghley
1572	- August 24, St Bartholomew's Day massacre in Paris where Huguenots were massacred en masse - Similar massacres happened elsewhere in France - This caused widespread panic in England and fear of invasion by the Catholics
1573	- Dec 21- Sir Francis Walsingham is chosen Principal Secretary of State and also becomes Elizabeth's chief spy master

1575	-	Nov 14- Queen Elizabeth refused to recognize the Netherlands as a sovereign state
1577	-	A coalition is shaped between England and Netherlands
	-	Francis Drake becomes the first Englishmen to navigate around the world. He renames his ship from Pelican to the Golden Hind
1578	-	Mar 10- Queen Elizabeth consents to sending aid of 20,000 pounds to the Dutch
	-	Sep 21- Robert Dudley, the Queen's favorite, in secret weds Lady Lettice Knollys at Wanstead
1579	-	Jun 17- Sir Francis Drake claims a new territory for the crown to be called New Albion, where California is now
	-	Aug 17- Francis, Duke of Anjou, visits Queen Elizabeth at Greenwich hoping to wed her
	-	Oct 7, 1579 - The Privy Council redacts their support for Queen Elizabeth as a result of the marriage contract with the Duke of Anjou
1580	-	Sep 26- Francis Drake triumphantly returns home to England
1581	-	Nov 7- A treaty of marriage is signed between Queen Elizabeth and the Duke of Anjou
1584	-	William of Orange is murdered. The Queen again sends money to Holland
	-	Mar 25- Walter Raleigh receives royal admission to travel around and start a settlement within North America.
	-	Jun 4 – Walter Raleigh establishes a colony in Virginia known as Roanoke Island.
	-	Jun 15 - Francis, Duke of Anjou dies
1585	-	Jun 29- Queen Elizabeth declines offers by the Dutch commission for sovereignty of the Low Countries
	-	Aug 14- Queen Elizabeth declares total

	-	protection of Holland for as long as she reigns.
	-	Dec 8 – Dudley is acting general for the English army as they go to drive the Spanish troops out of Holland.
1586	-	The Babbington Plot - Sir Francis Walsingham finds out a secret plan to murder the Queen
	-	Jul 1- Treaty of Berwick - Queen Elizabeth and James VI of Scotland create a league for mutual protection and benefit
	-	Oct. 25 - Mary, Queen of Scots, is tried and convicted due to her intent to assassinate the Queen.
1587	-	February 8- Mary is executed.
	-	England and Spain declare war upon one another.
1587	-	Apr 19 - Drake terminates the Spanish fleet at Cadiz
	-	Jun 18- Queen Elizabeth appoints the Earl of Essex, Robert Devereux, to be her Master of the Horse
1588	-	Aug. 8- The Spanish Armada of 132 ships is defeated by the English Royal Navy of 34 ships and 163 armed merchant vessels, minting the English Navy a powerhouse.
	-	Sep 4- Robert Dudley succumbs to death.
1591	-	Apr 10- James Lancaster sails over to Plymouth in search for new province and lands.
	-	Apr 17- Queen Elizabeth gives aid to France.
1592	-	Thomas Cavendish, English sailor and explorer dies
	-	January 30 – Pope Innocent IX dies.
	-	Ippolito Aldobrandini is elected Pope Clement VIII.
1593	-	The London Theatres close because of the rampant plague.
	-	Queen Elizabeth tells Parliament that she has the right to agree or disagree with any

	decision they make. - Penalties are imposed on those who choose not to attend Church services. - Attending Catholic Mass becomes illegal.
1597	- Large-scale Irish rebellion - King Philip II of Spain decides to send yet another armada in an attempt to take over England, but heavy storms overthrow the ships. - Elizabeth elevates Robert Devereux's status from Earl of Essex to the Earl Marshal of England
1599	- Robert signs a secret truce with the Earl of Tyrone in an act of incredible rebellion - Queen Elizabeth removes Essex of his honors and calls for his arrest
1600	- Queen Elizabeth I awards a charter to East India Company
1601	- Elizabethan Poor Law delegates the responsibility of providing for the poor to the Parishes. - Earl of Essex attempts a major rebellion - 25th February-Robert Devereux is executed on Tower Green
1603	- Death of Queen Elizabeth on 24 March 1603 as a result of blood poisoning - James I of England, James VI of Scotland, succeeds her as heir and is proclaimed King. - This ends the Tudor dynasty and begins the Stuart Monarchy.

Chapter 6- The Legacy of Queen Elizabeth I

"It would please me best if, at last, a marble stone shall record that this Queen having lived such and such a time, lived and died a virgin."

Elizabeth's legacy is admired both as a woman, a ruler, a Queen and above all, someone who rose above all stigma and juxtaposition. From birth till the end of her life, Elizabeth broke boundaries and created new ways of doing things, while at the same time changing perceptions and changing England to become the modern country that it was destined to be.

Elizabeth held on her shoulders proudly the immense history of the Tudor monarchy and, indeed, proved herself to be the greatest of the Tudors during her 45-year reign.

Growing up a motherless child, Elizabeth was also surrounded with the understanding and knowledge that her father married and divorced his six wives, and also beheaded some of them. Surrounded with this information, one can only deduce why Elizabeth was not so eager to be married herself.

However, Elizabeth I knew exactly why a Queen would marry. But despite the pressures she faced, she apparently did not think to marry a man was that important.

Due to her virgin status, she was also known as 'The Virgin Queen.'

Elizabeth's legacy created a lasting impact especially in these areas:

- She unified and created a religious settlement that created the foundations for the Church of England to become an established religion and faith center in the country.

- She pushed forward tolerance and ruling by consent, a theme never practiced by her predecessors. It set the precedence for future kings and queens of England to rule upon.

- She created a compromise that allowed both Protestants and Catholics to pray and continue their beliefs. Although it took a while for people to accept this and be comfortable with the idea, the very fact that Elizabeth I spearheaded this move showed that she was a Queen ahead of her time.

- During her reign, exploration and trade increased partly due to Elizabeth's openness to exploring the wider world. England turned from a minor player to a major world power during her reign.

- Her love of the arts and theater encouraged the expansion and interests in the arts. English theater became more prominent during this time, especially with the memorable and lasting creations of William Shakespeare.

Women even in the 21st century face pressures of getting married, as it is seen as a natural path to womanhood and adulthood. To go through this back then, and even more so as a Queen, one has to admire her courage and forthrightness to stay grounded and firm to be a female first above all.

Elizabeth was also the first Tudor ruler to recognize the importance of consent and held strongly to the belief that a monarch must have popular consent to rule its kingdom.

Elizabeth surrounded herself with loyal advisors - people that she could trust and whose advice she valued and drew strength from. This is a value that the subsequent Stuart monarchy failed to follow.

Elizabeth trusted in God, honest advice from her tight-knit and very smart council, and had immense love for her people.

Elizabeth has been quoted as *saying "when wars and seditions with grievous persecutions have vexed almost all kings and countries round about me, my reign hath been peaceable, and my realm a receptacle to thy afflicted Church. The love of my people hath appeared firm, and the devices of my enemies frustrate"*.

When Elizabeth had finally succumbed to death, men of her court removed and examined her jewelry. In a locket ring on the finger of her left hand, they found two miniature portraits that were painted - one of herself and one of her mother, Anne Boleyn.

Elizabeth proved in that generation that women could indeed be great and powerful leaders, which would carve out an easier path, and also big shoes to fill, for future Queens.

Even in our modern day and age, Elizabeth's legacy continues to live on. She may be controversial in so many ways but she is always a renowned figure.

Following her death, historians, writers, poets, artists, and governments throughout the European realm celebrated her life, virtue, and reign.

Come the seventeenth century, Elizabeth's love life became a popular subject to the point of obsession in France and England and it inspired plenty of playwrights and operas.

In modern art and theater, the role of Elizabeth I has been portrayed by at least 30 actresses in films, television series, and movies. Not only that, she is also the recurring subject for many volumes of fact and fiction.

King Henry VIII may have wanted a male heir to continue his dynasty, but it is rather ironic to see that the person who succeeded most in ruling England was ultimately a woman. Queen Elizabeth broke the mold and became a shining example of empowerment at a time when women were considered unfit to rule, weak, or simple-minded.

From praising her leadership to lauding her love and patronage of the arts, or gossiping about her unwed status, Queen Elizabeth I remains an elusive woman, but endlessly compelling.

Conclusion

Once again, thank you for taking the time to read this book.

I hope you found it enjoyable and interesting to learn about the fascinating life of Queen Elizabeth I.

If you enjoyed this book, please take the time to leave a review on Amazon, it's greatly appreciated and helps me to continue producing books.

Also, don't forget to take a look at the other titles I have available on Amazon.

Once again, thank you, I truly hope you enjoyed reading this book!